CREATE YOUR OWN FASHION COLLECTION

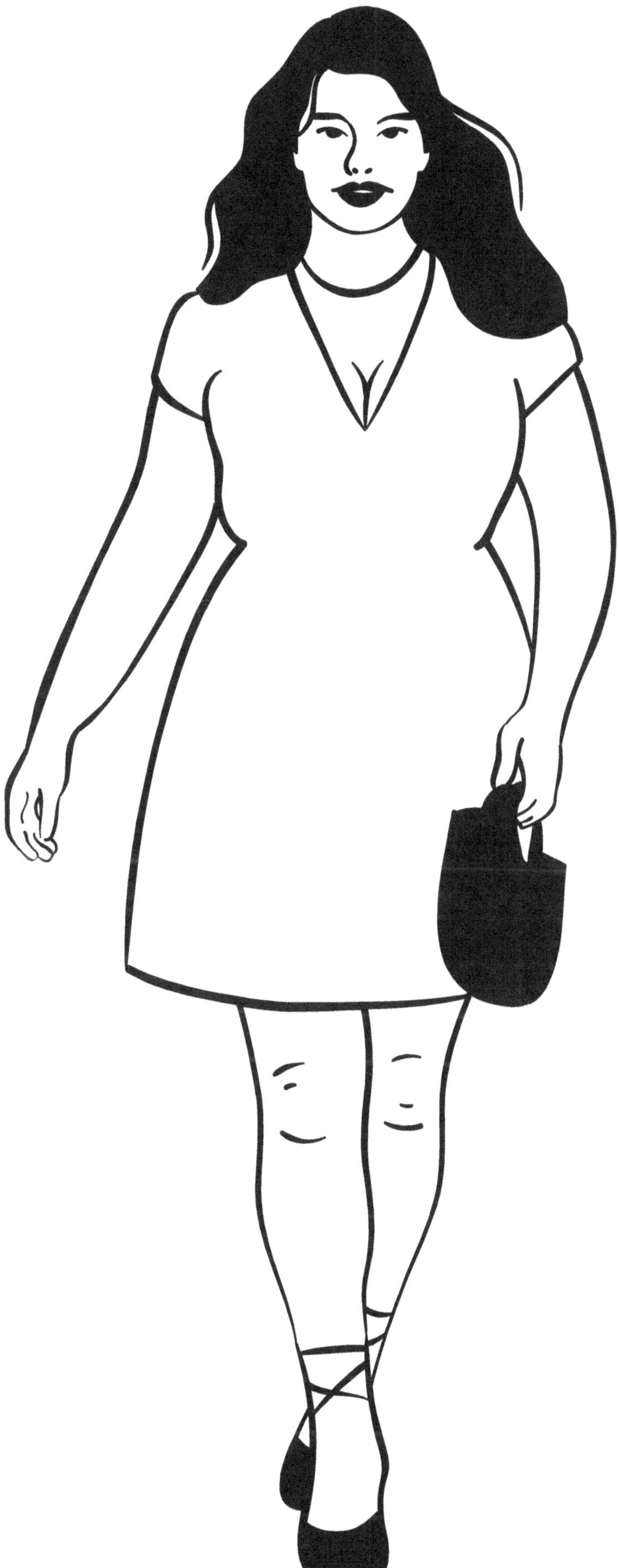

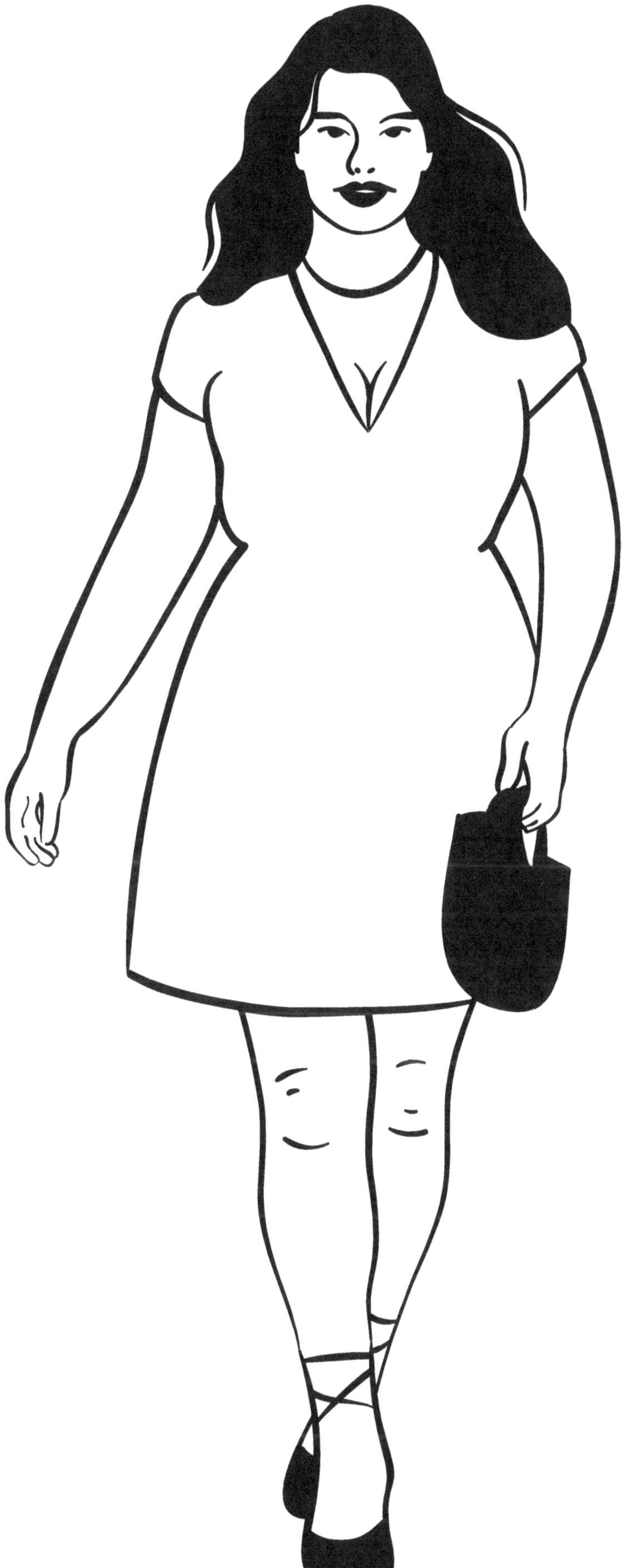

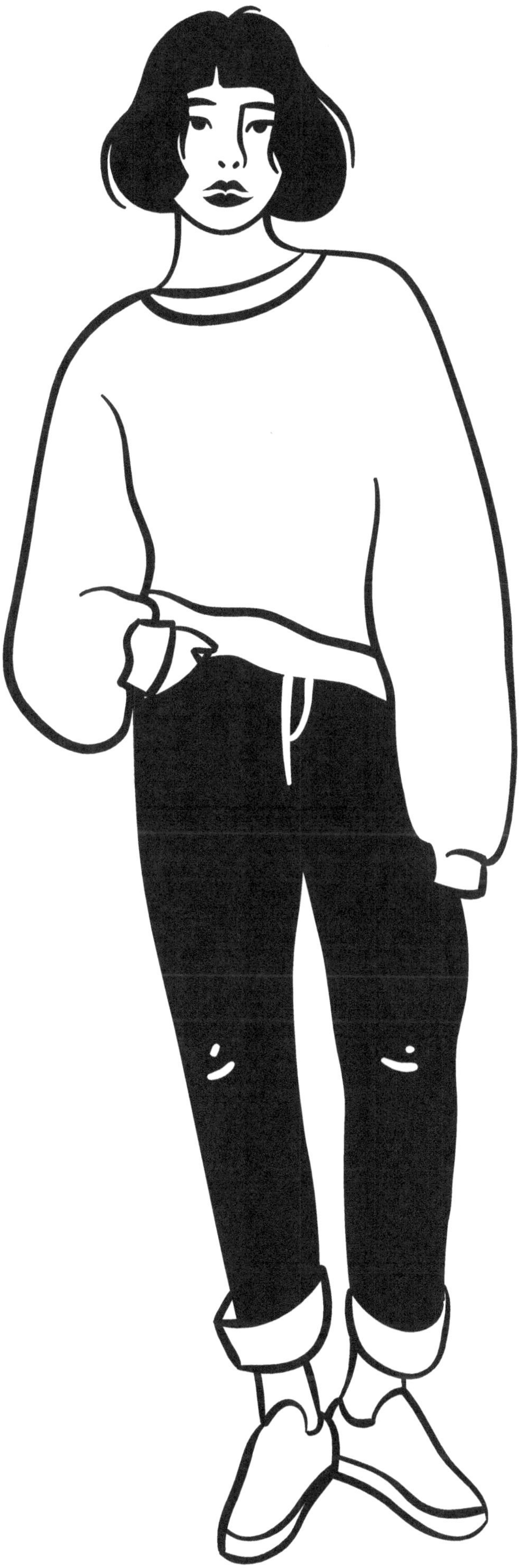

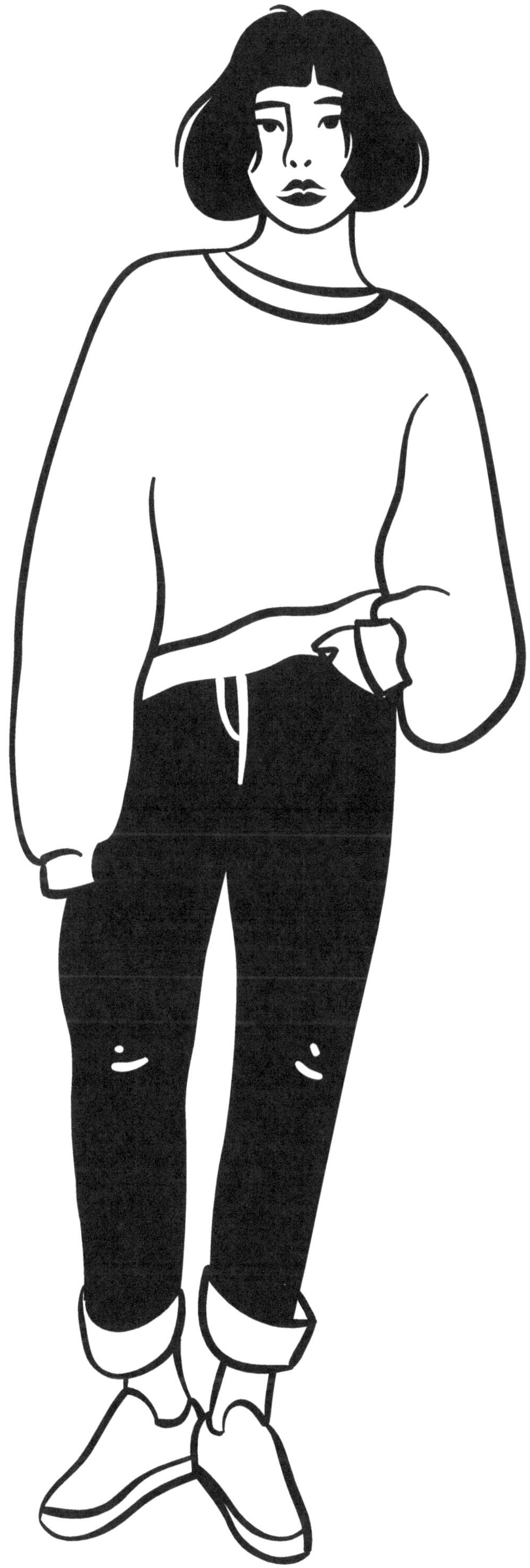

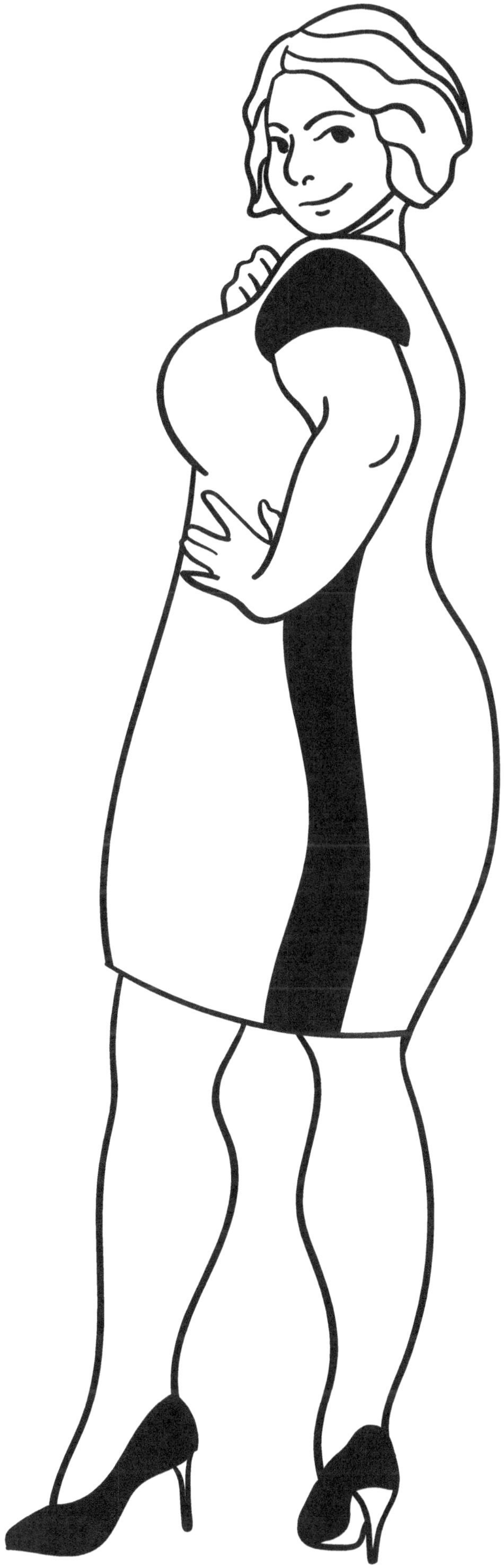

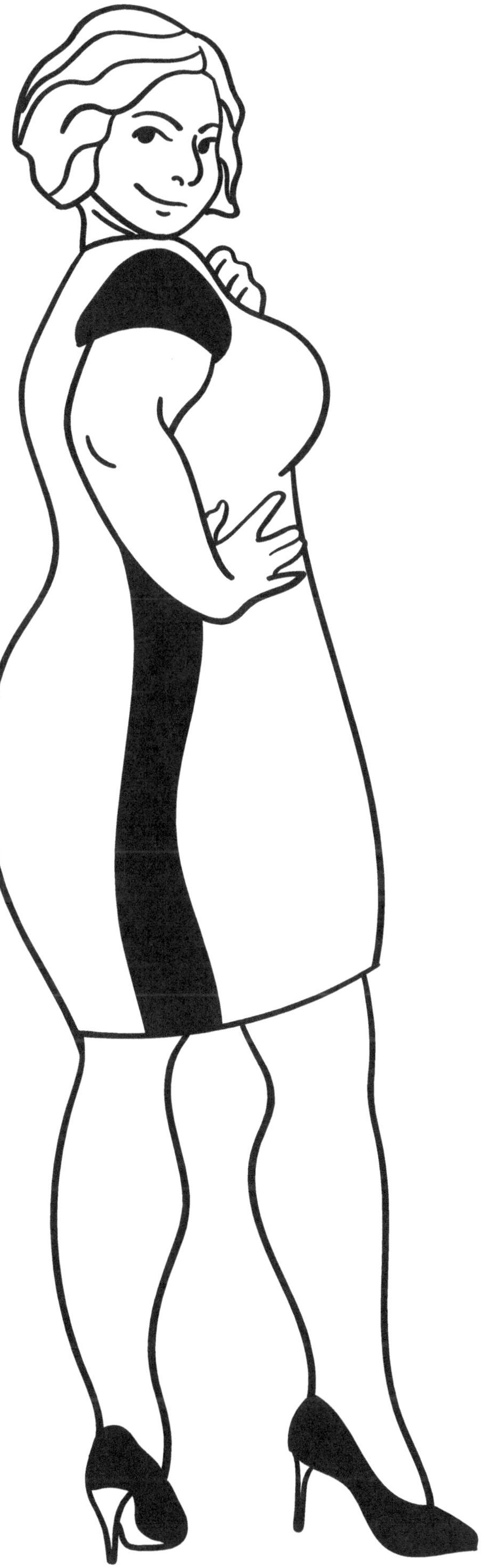

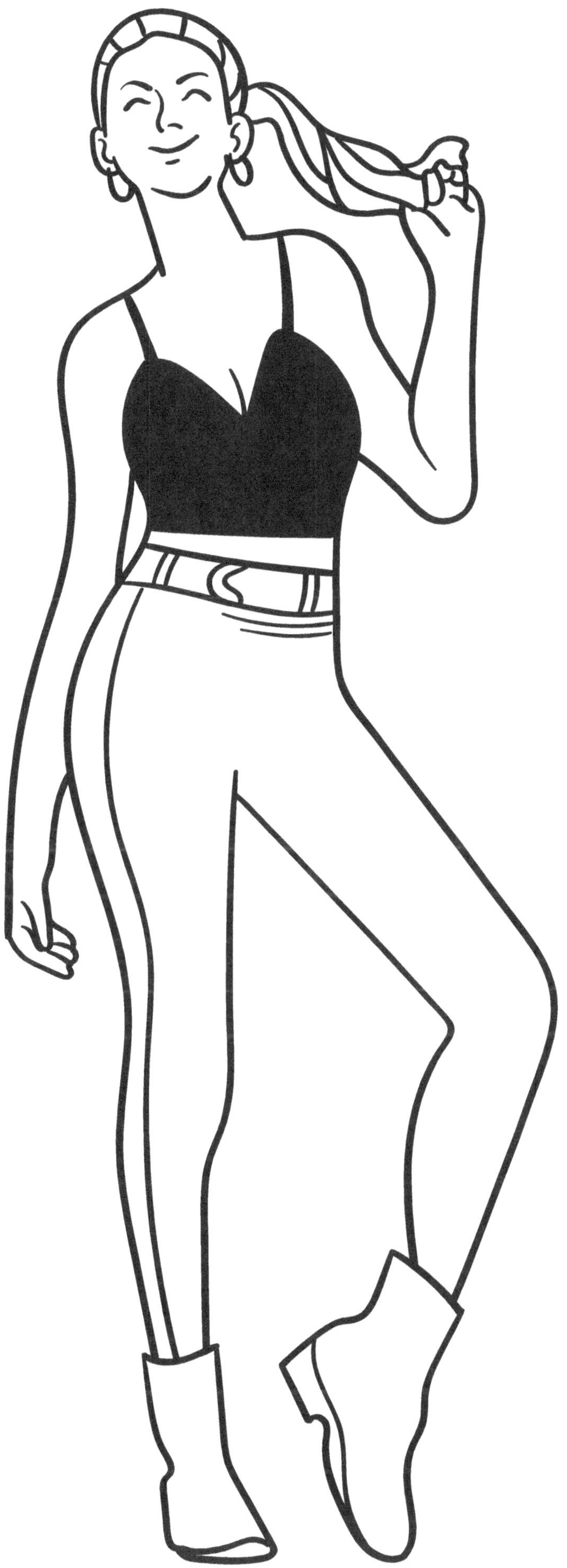

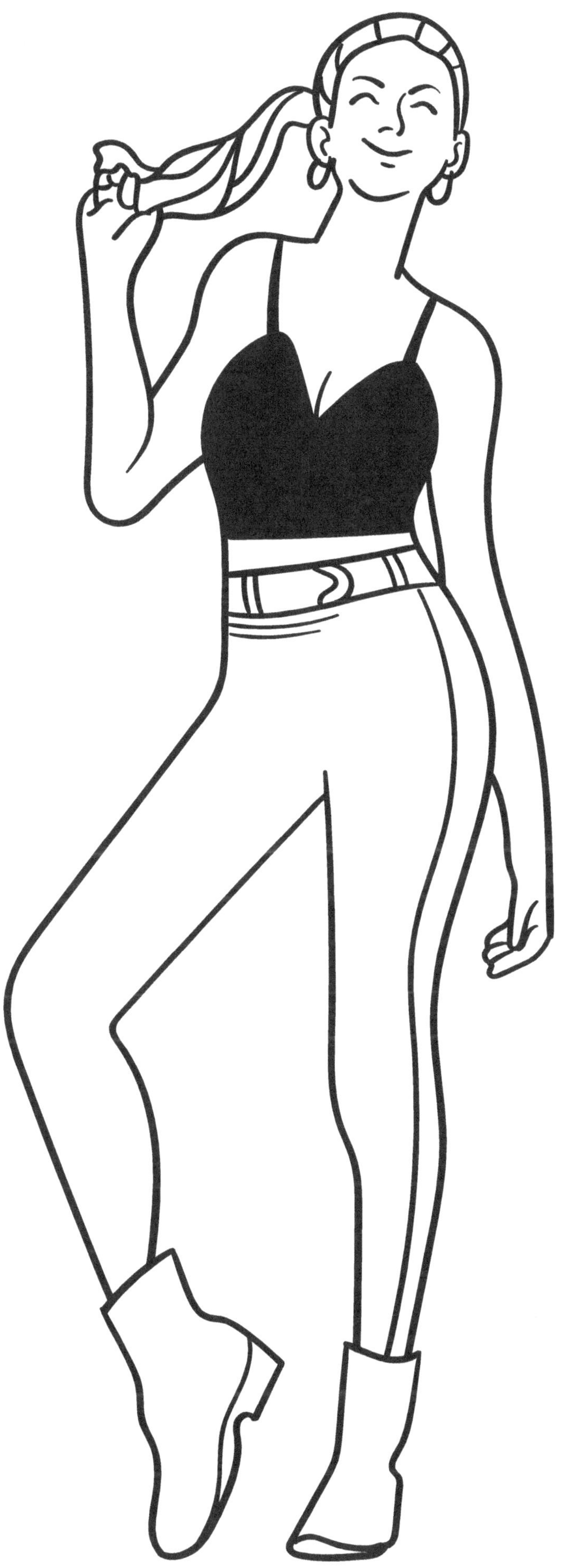

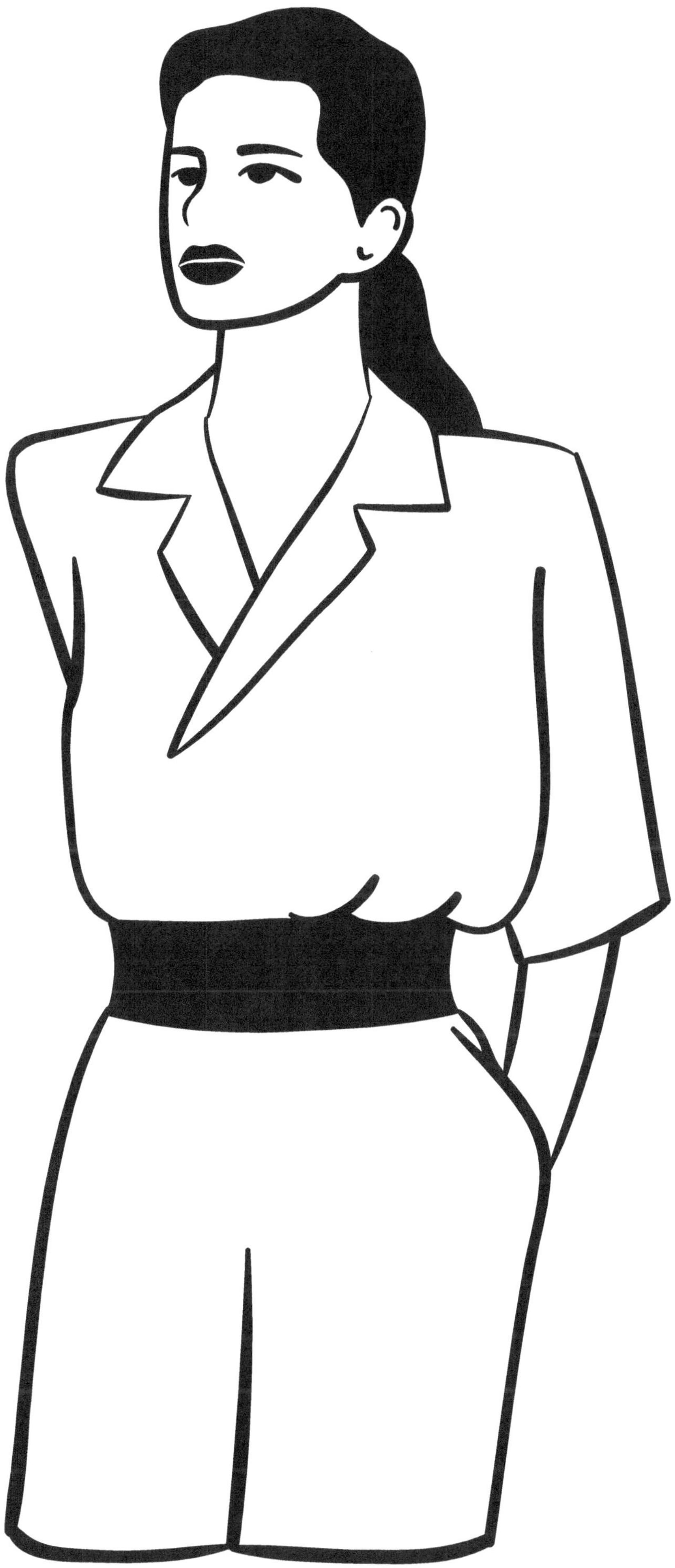

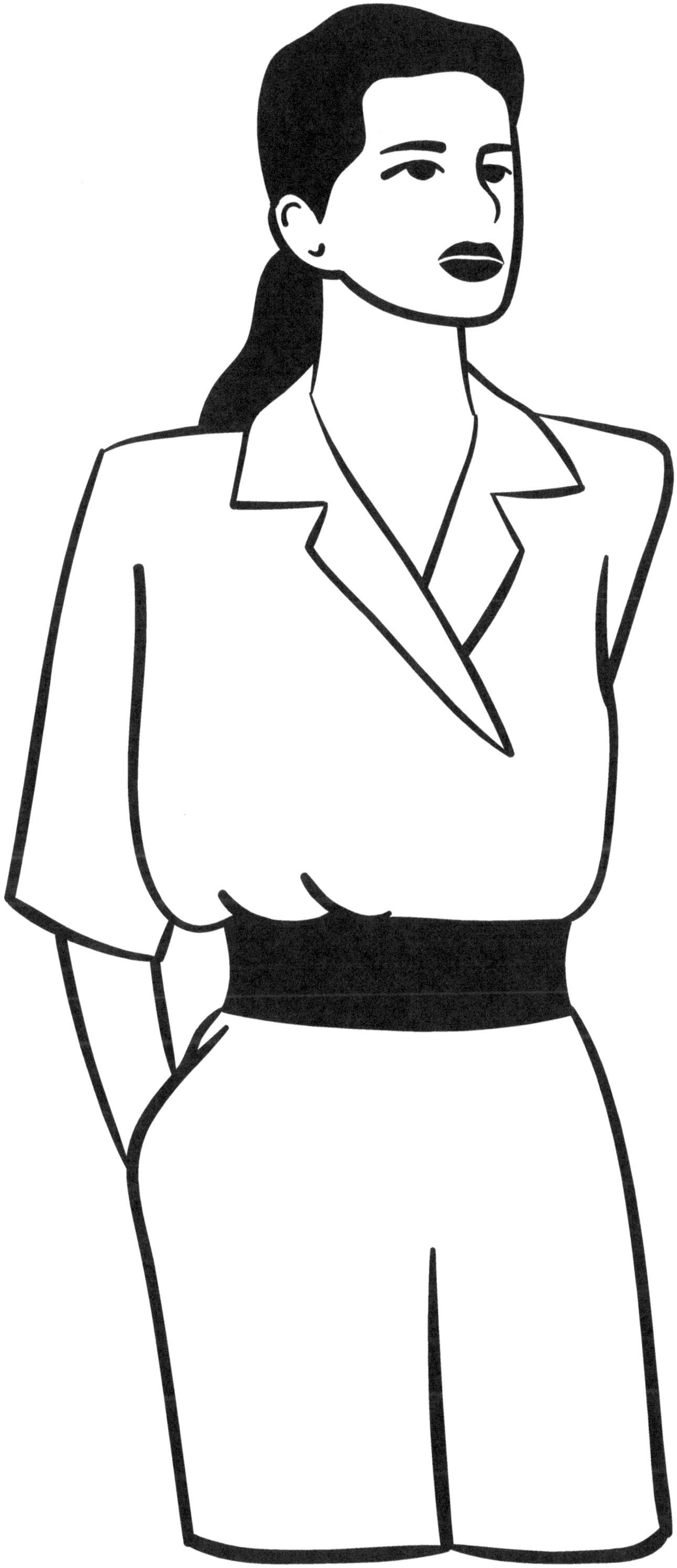

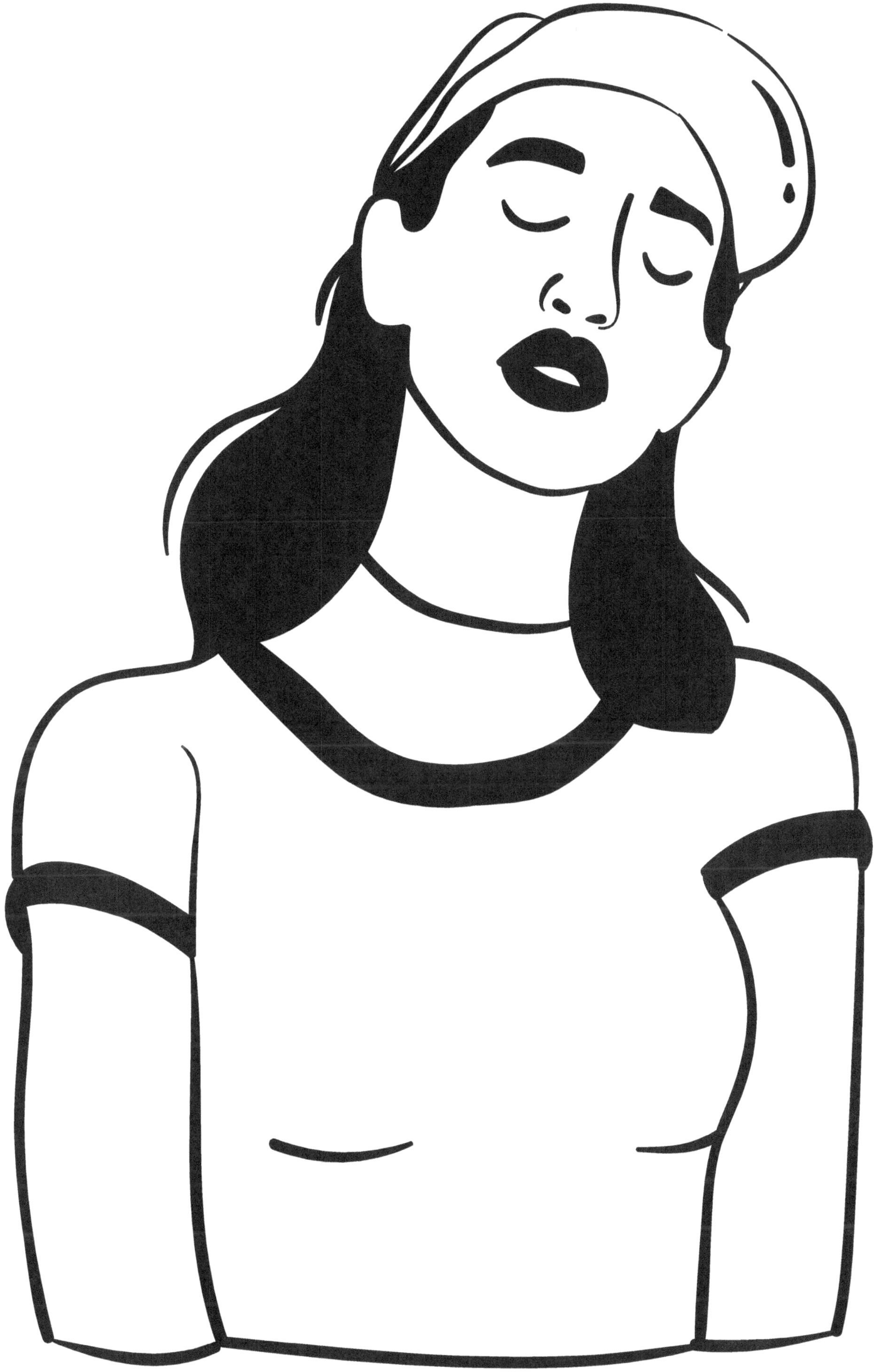

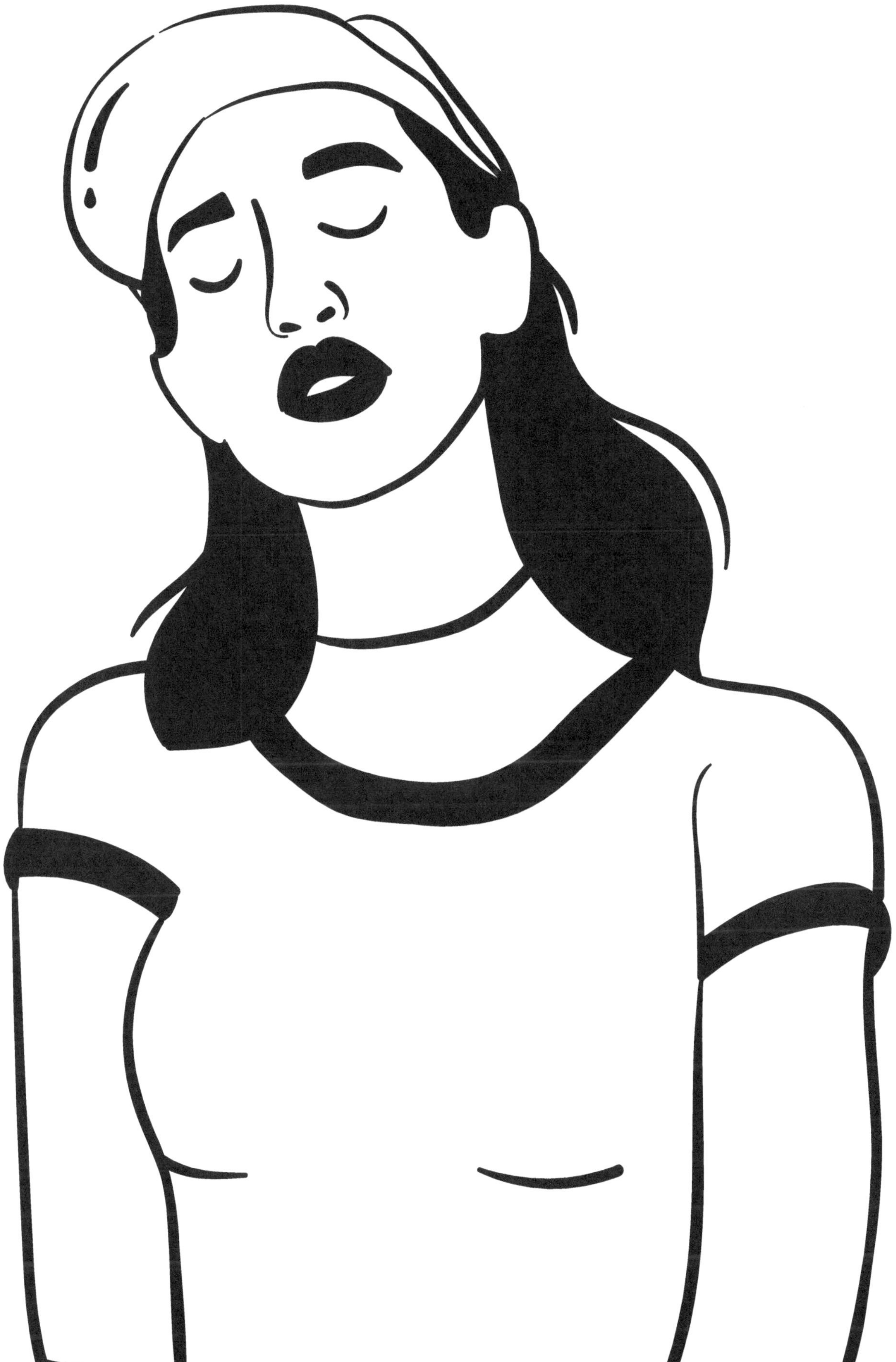

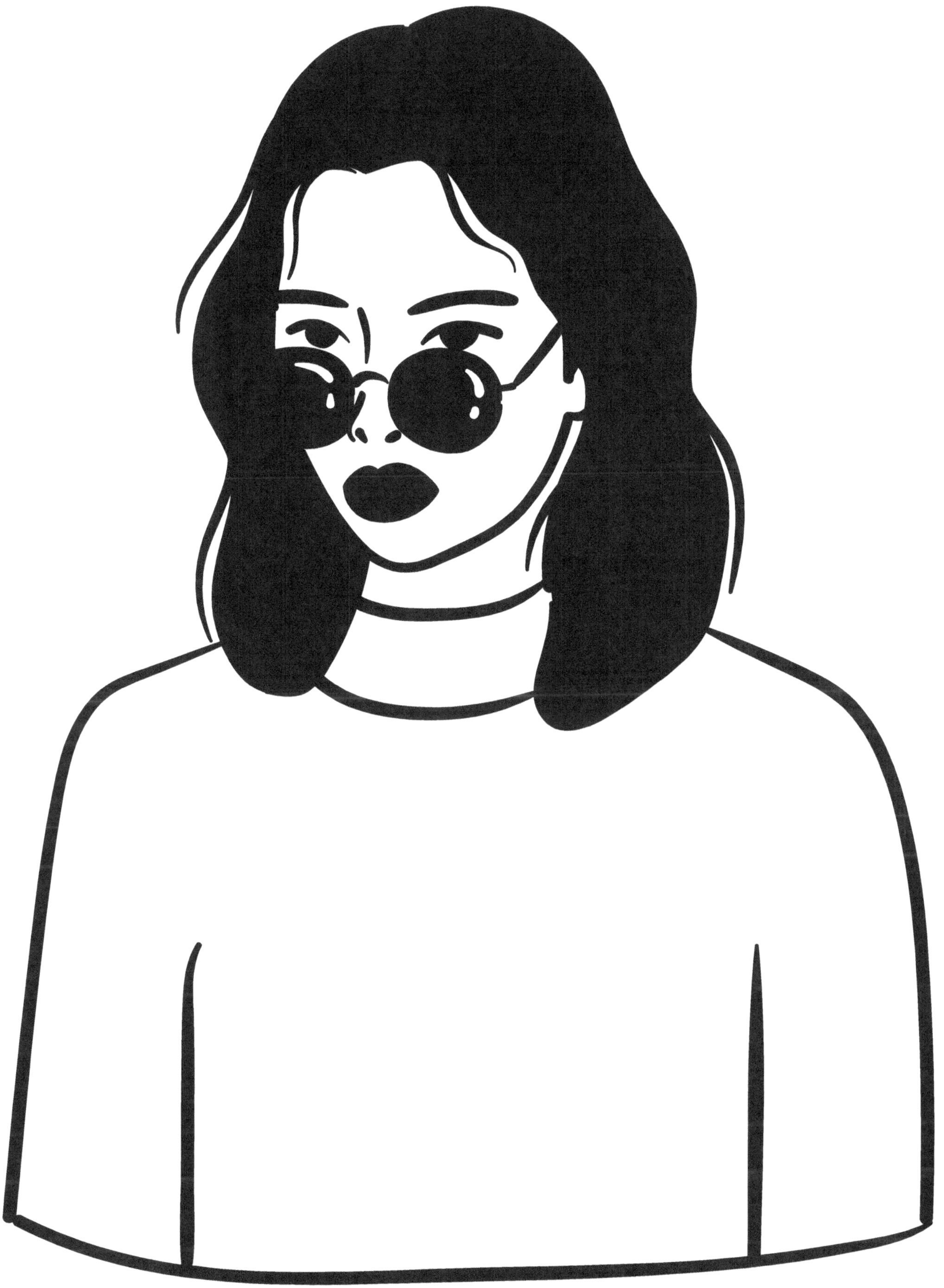

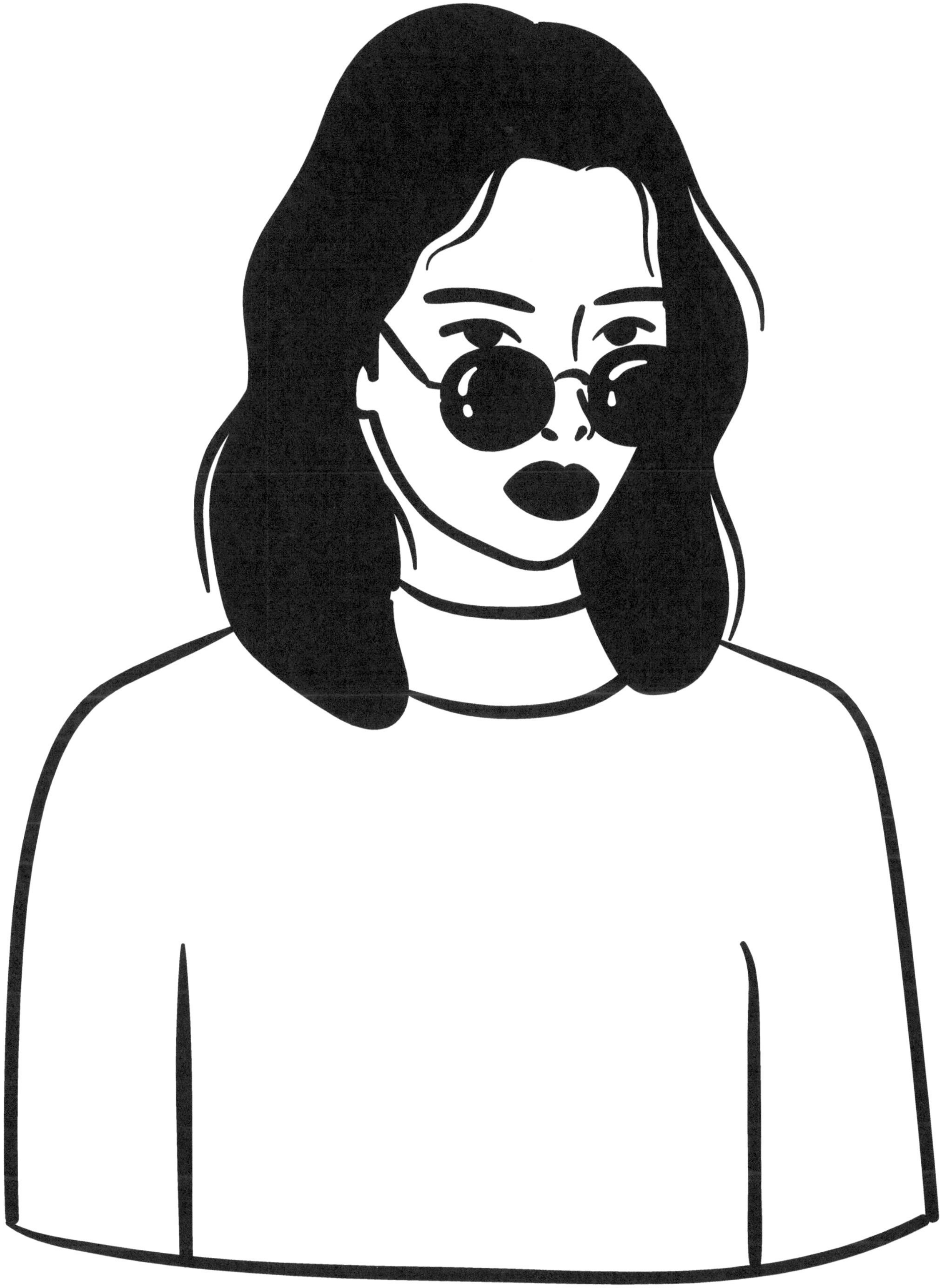

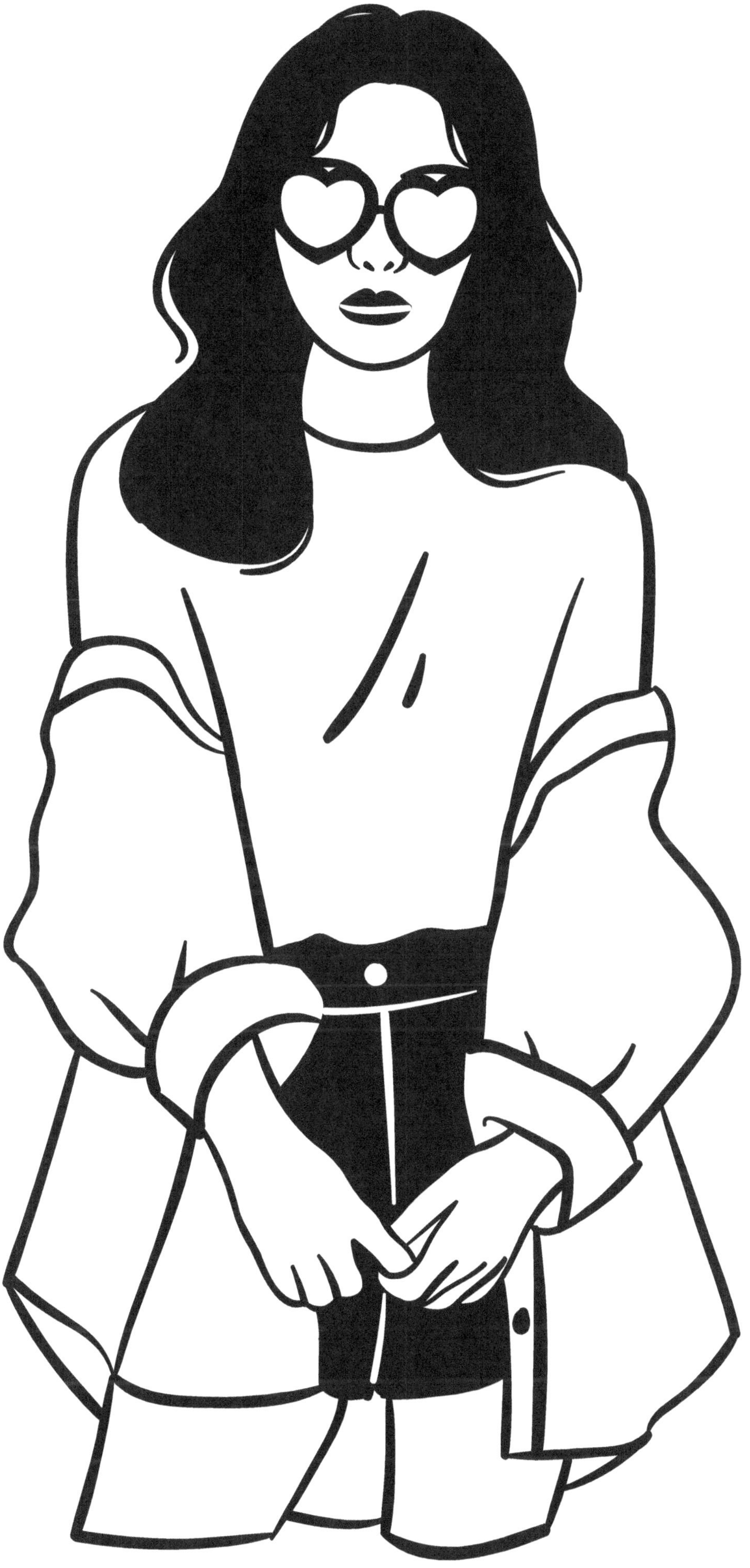

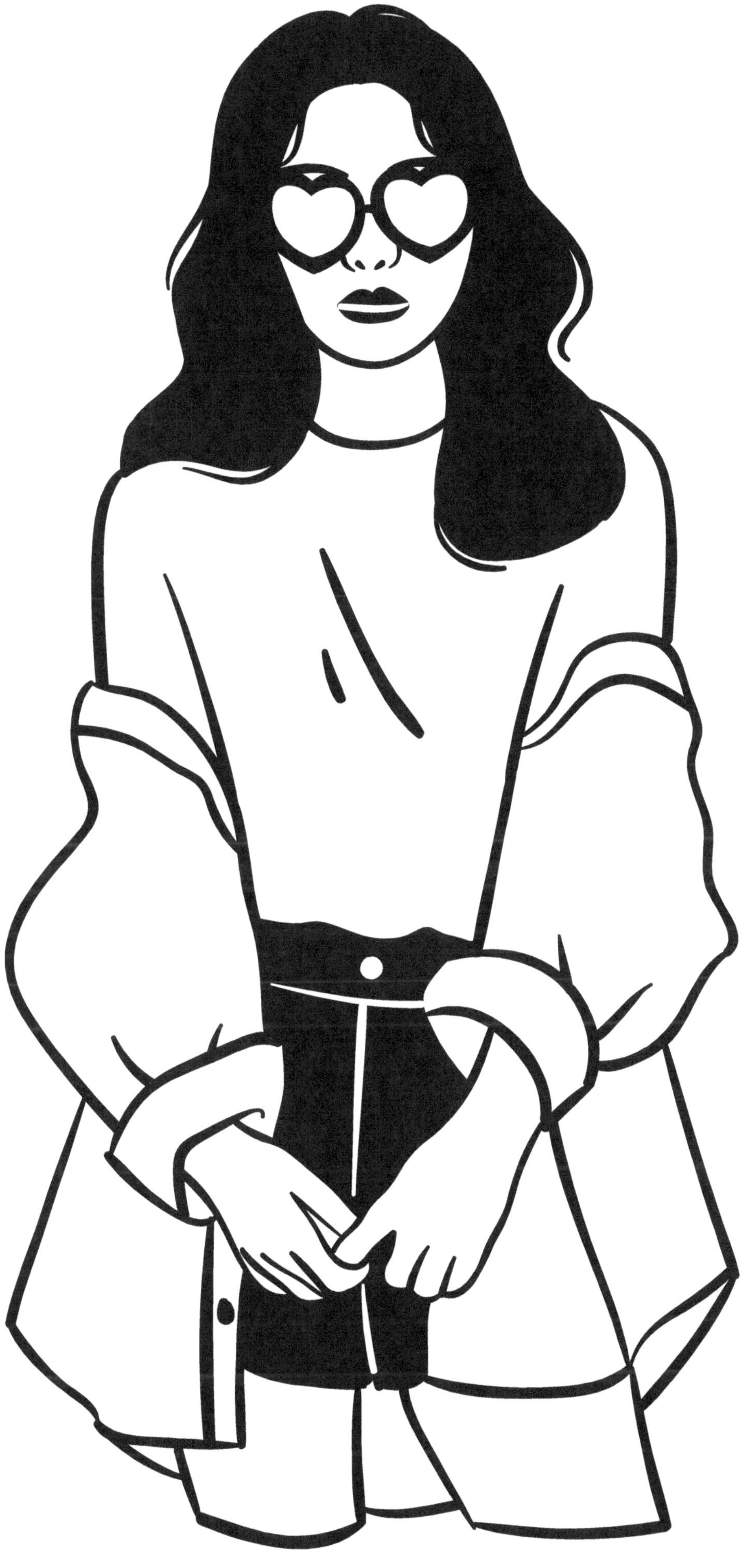

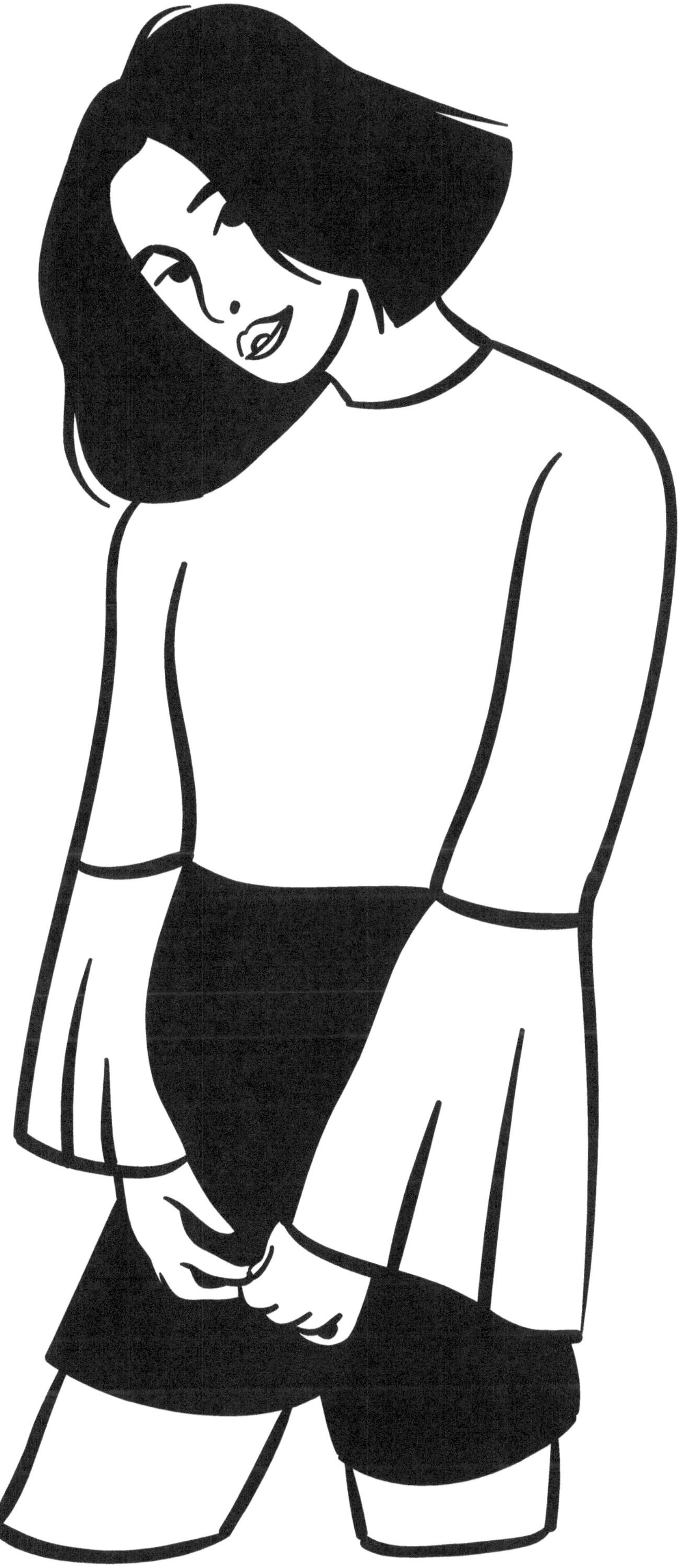

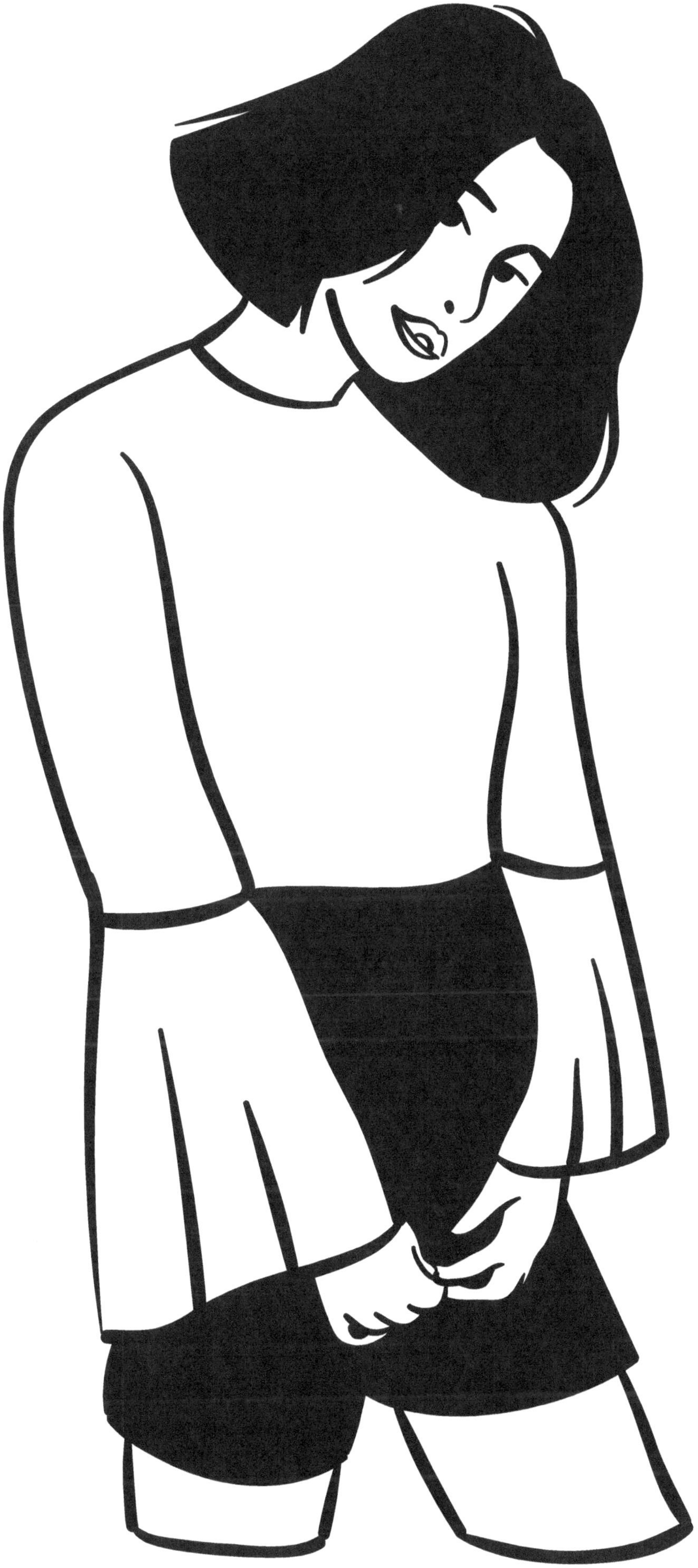

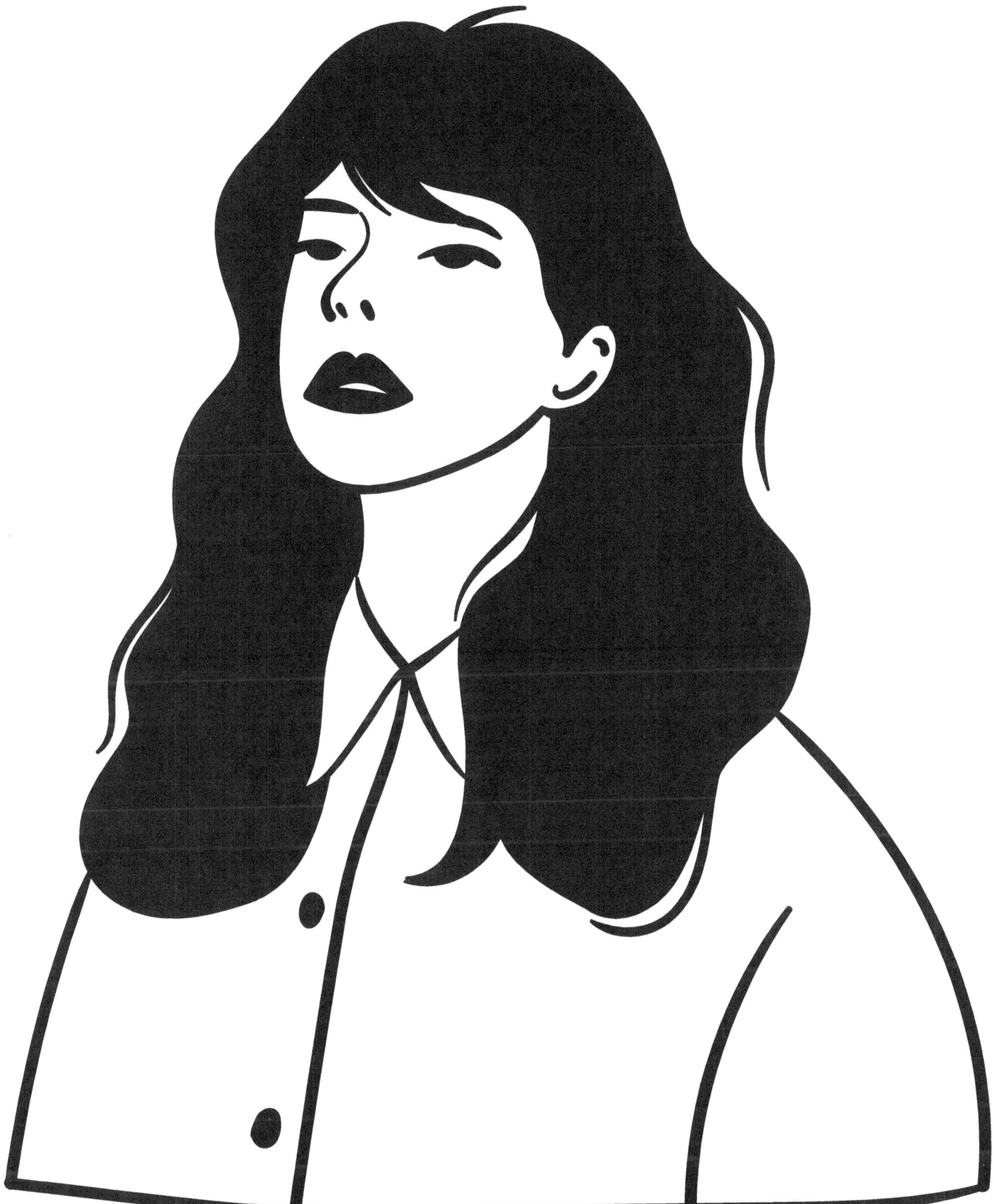

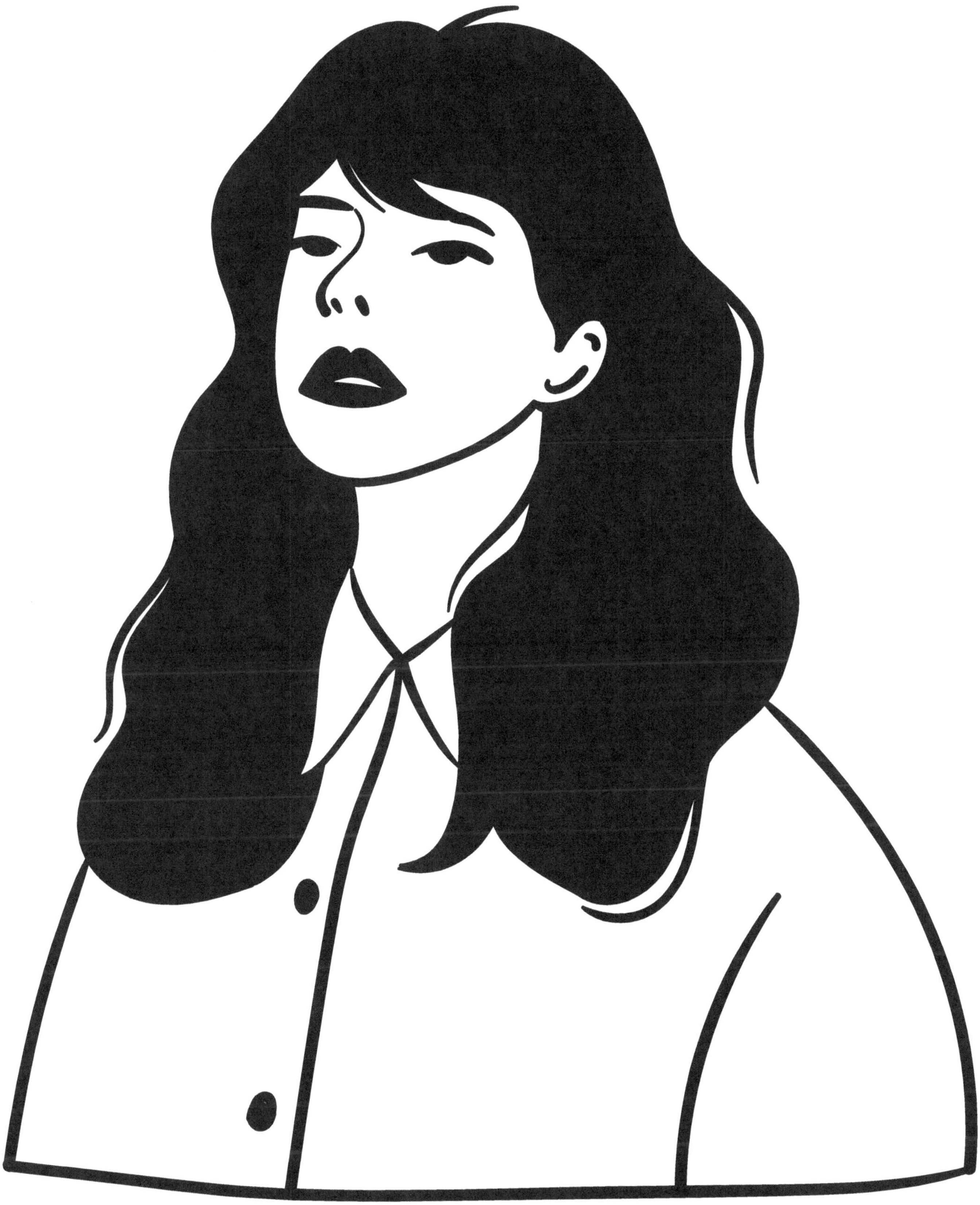

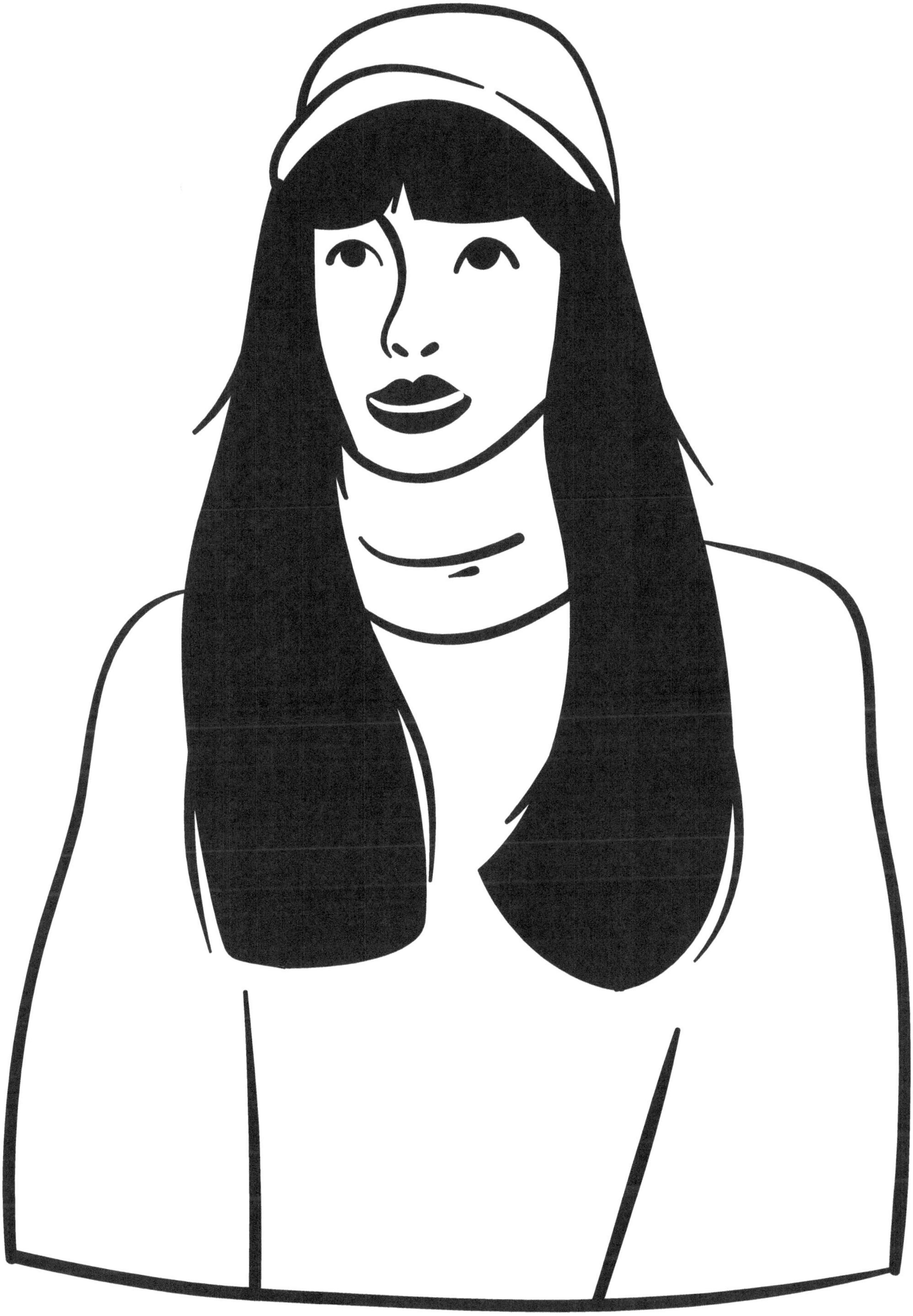

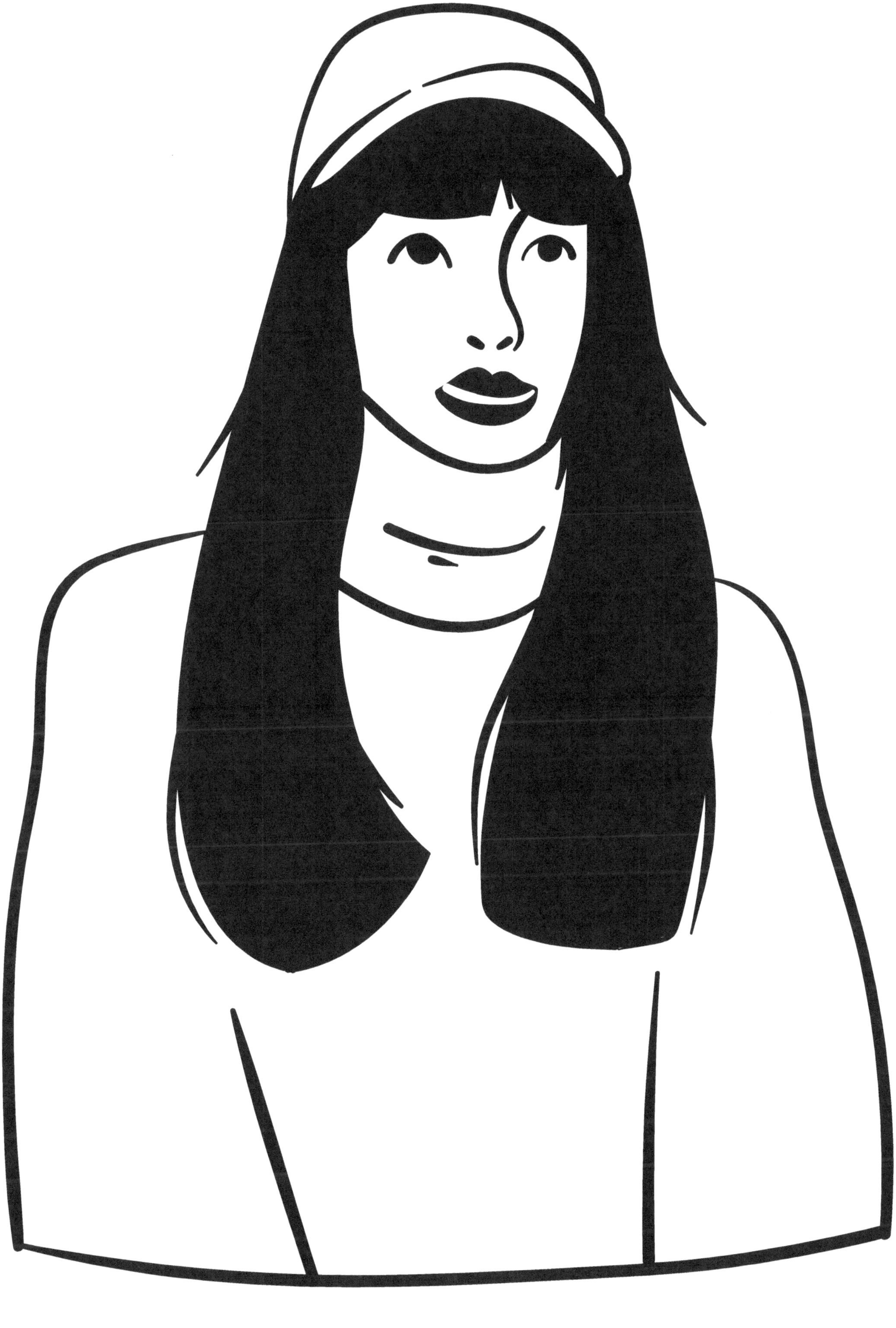

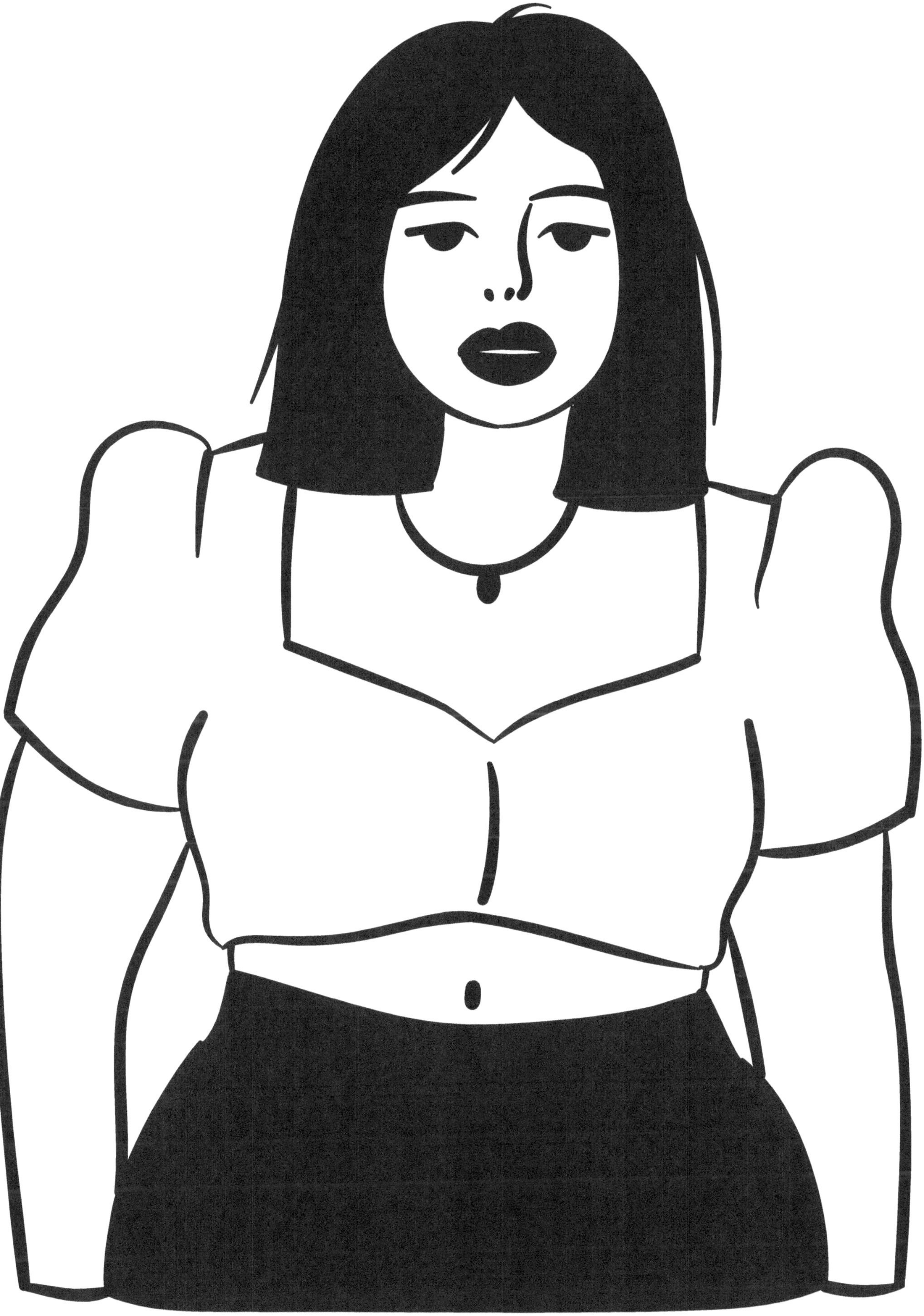

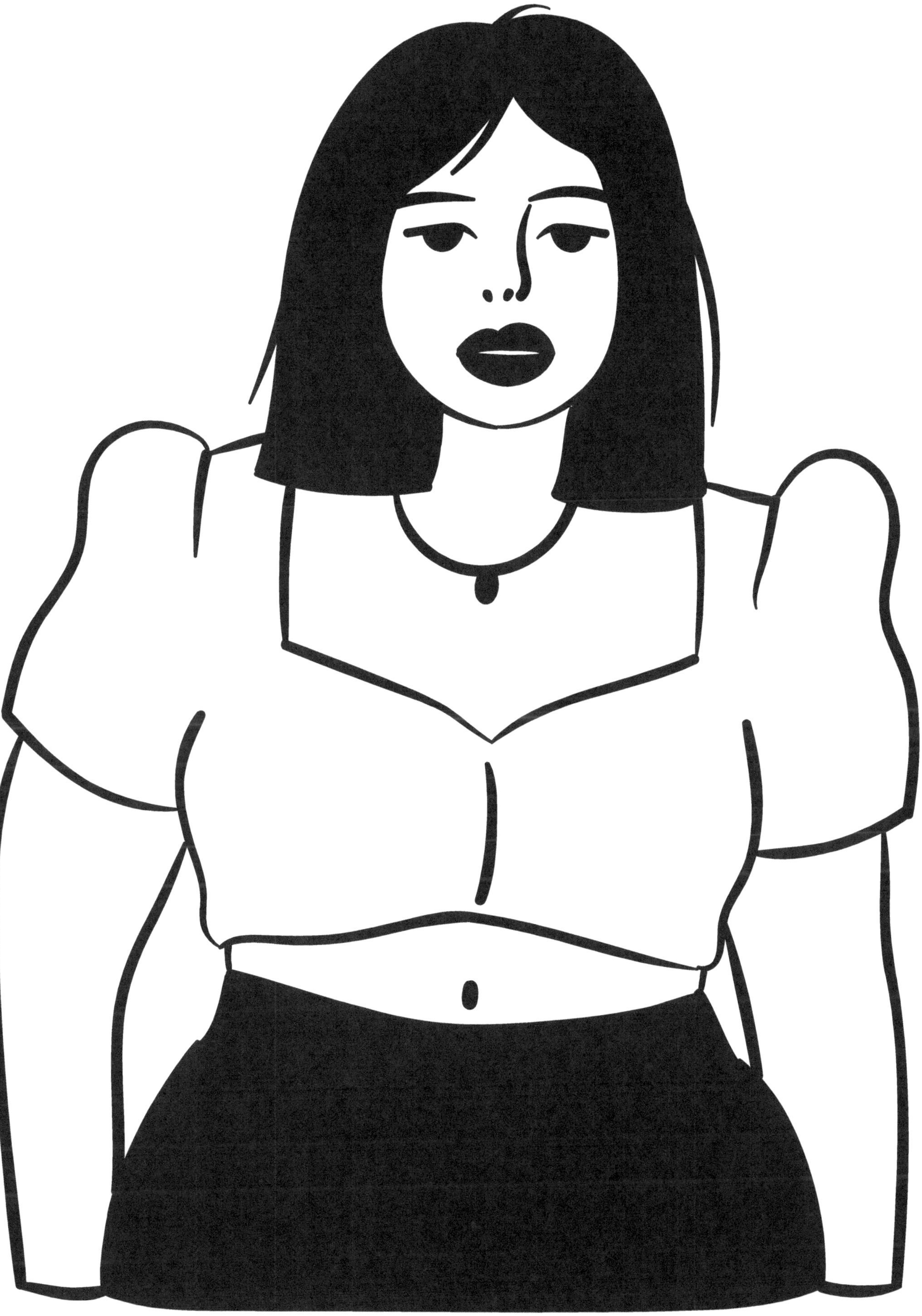

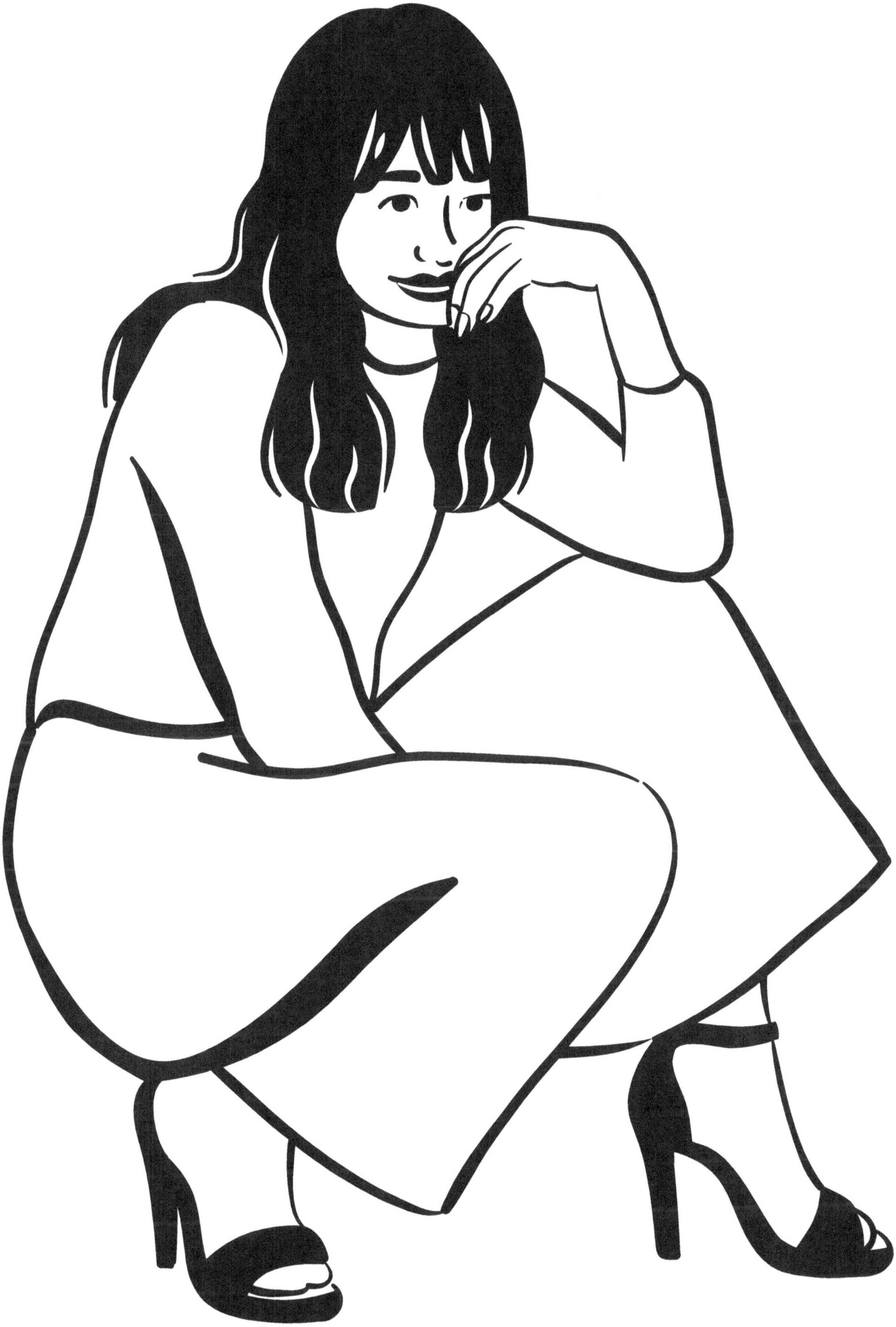

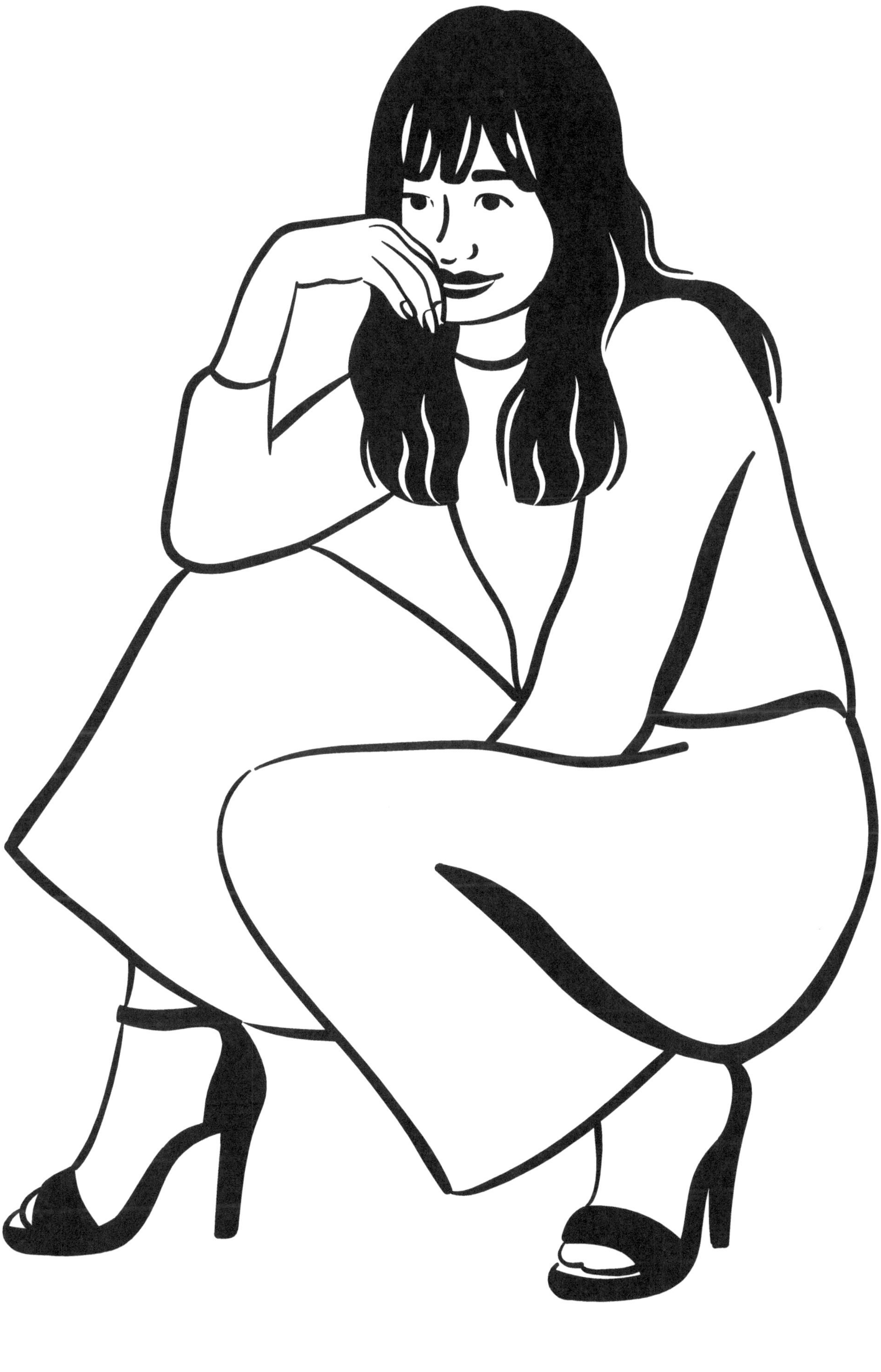

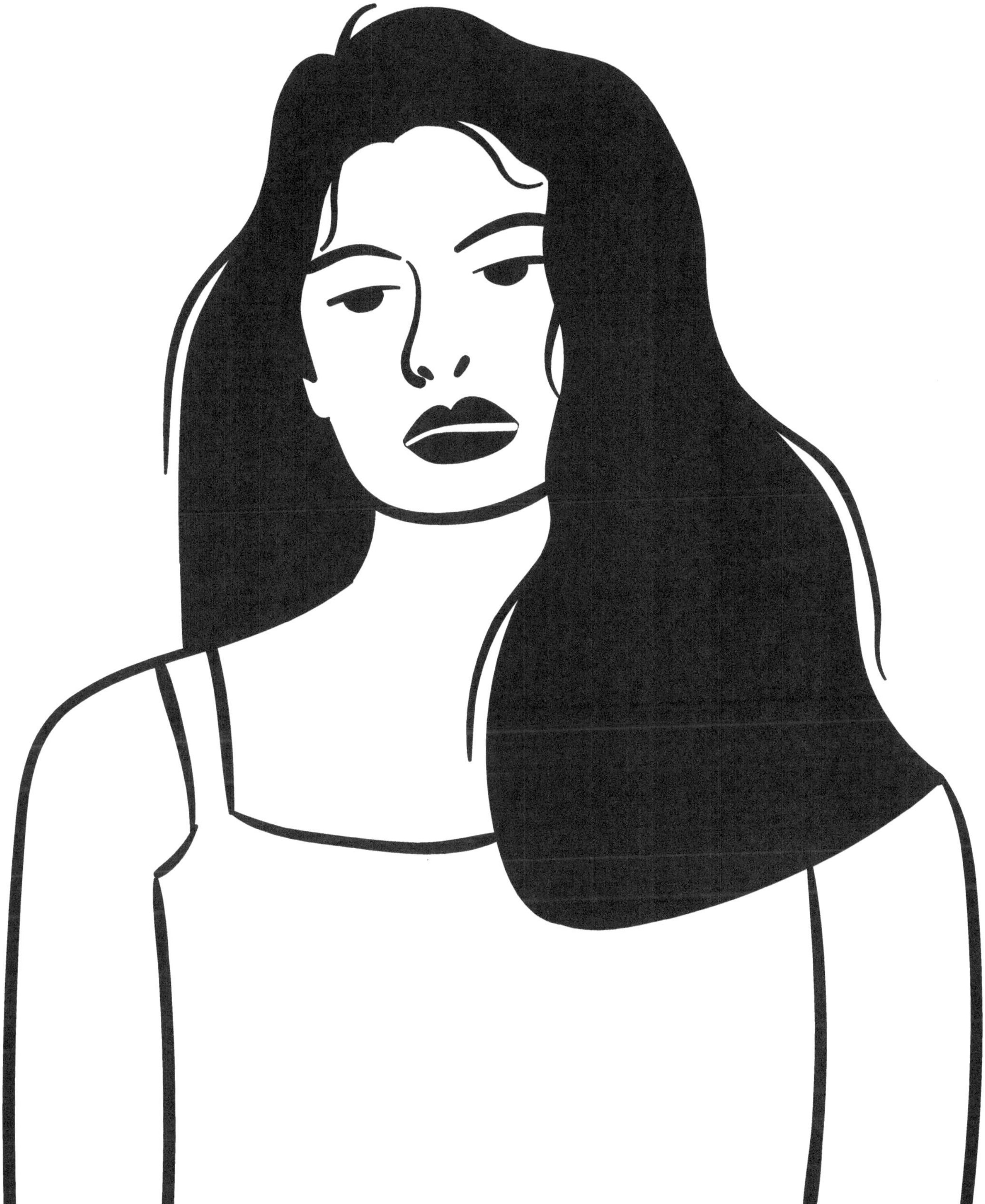

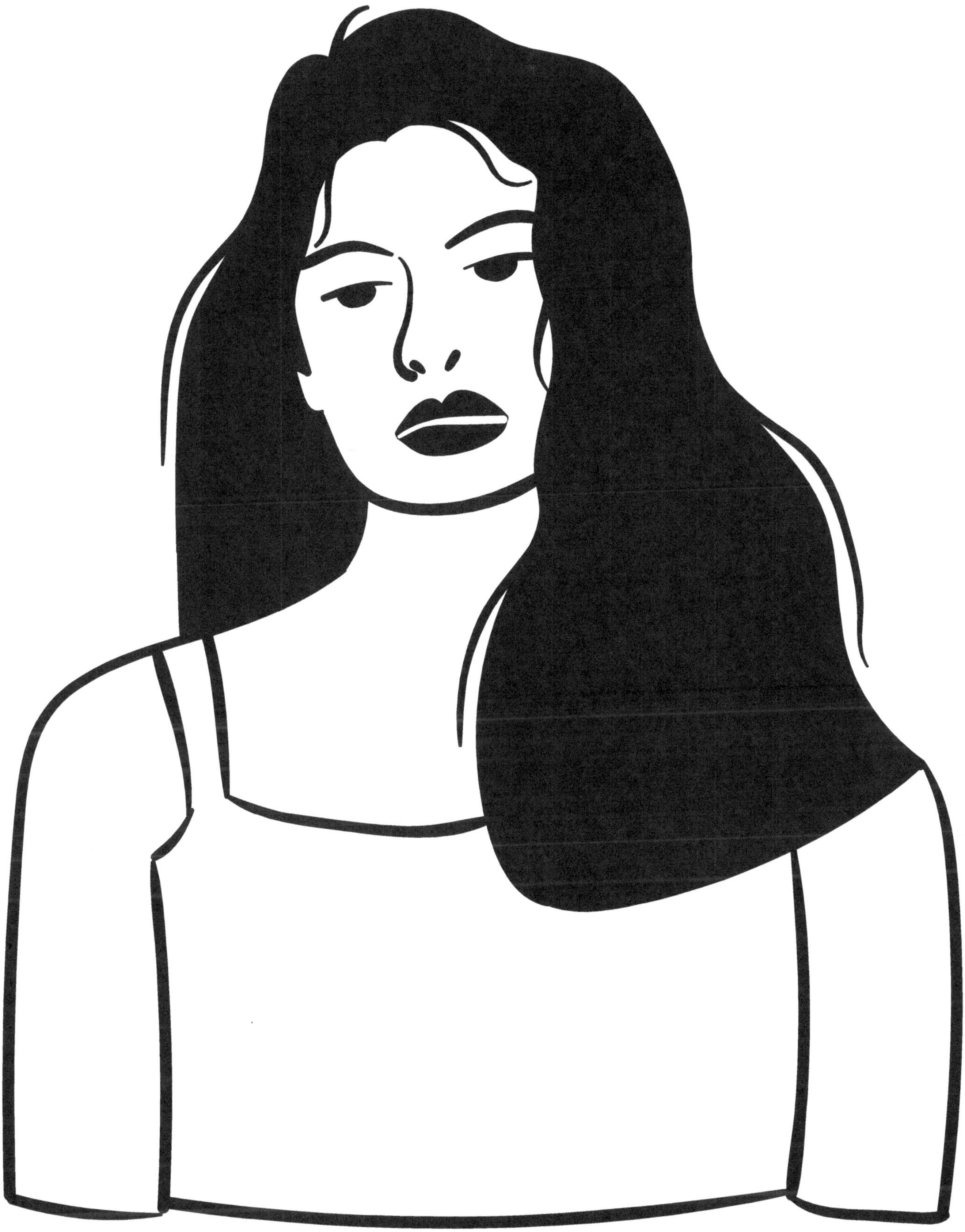

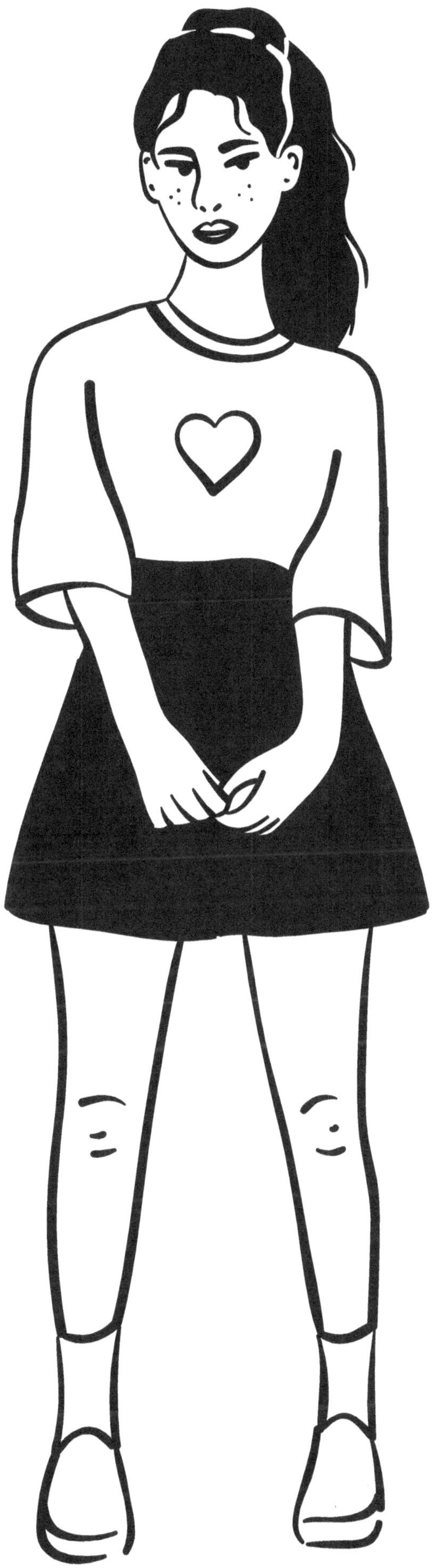

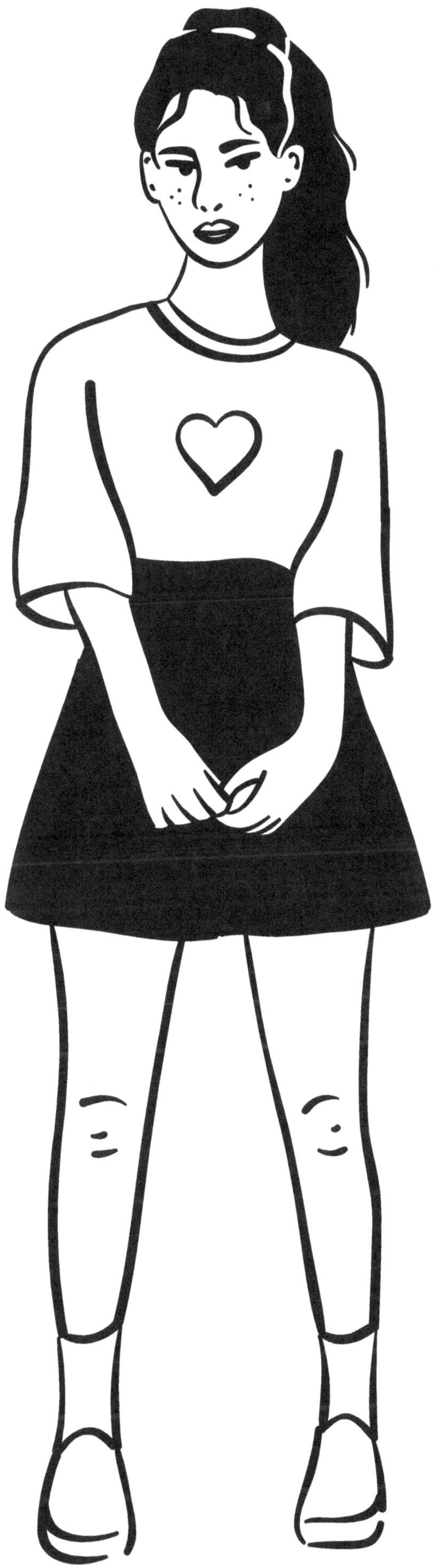

www.ingramcontent.com/pod-product-compliance
Lightning Source LLC
Chambersburg PA
CBHW081000220526
45467CB00008B/2638
9798683743628